DISCOVER&
LEARN

ENVIRONMENTAL
ISSUES

by

Holly Duhig

Photocredits

Abbreviations: l-left, r-right, b-bottom, t-top, c-centre, m-middle.

Front Cover - Aleksey Stemmer. 2 - D'July. 4tl - PhotoSky. 4tm - taviphoto. 4tr - Eric Isselee. 4b - Shchipkova Elena. 5 - Travel landscapes background. 6 - Maggy Meyer. 7t - Tei Sinthip. 7b - Sanne vd Berg Fotografie. 8 - Canon Boy. 9 - Seb c'est bien. 10 - javarman. 11tr - Smileus. 11tl - nattanan726. 11br - Eric Isselee. 11bl - Rudmer Zwerver. 12 - Edwin Butter. 13 - Andreas R.. 14 - davemhuntphotography. 15 - Brandon Alms. 16 - Dirk Ercken. 17 - Rosa Jay. 18 - Shane Gross. 19 - Vangert. 19inset - Hintau Aliaksei. 20 - Willyam Bradberry. 21 - Jacqueline Lee. 22 - RZwa. 23 - Lee319. 24 - Neale Cousland. 25 - Martin Mecnarowski. 26 - Ondrej Prosicky. 27 - Kletr. 28 - Christian Vinces. 29 - Sebastian Janicki. 30 - FikMik. Images are courtesy of Shutterstock.com. With thanks to Getty Images, Thinkstock Photo and iStockphoto.

©2017
Book Life
King's Lynn
Norfolk PE30 4LS

ISBN: 978-1-78637-158-4

Written by:
Holly Duhig

Edited by:
Charlie Ogden

Designed by:
Drue Rintoul

CONTENTS

Words in **bold** are explained in the glossary on page 31.

WHAT IS
THE ENVIRONMENT?

The environment is everything in the world around us. This includes the air, earth, water and **climate**, as well as the **natural** resources that exist on planet Earth. The environment also includes living things such as plants and animals.

Natural resources are things in the environment that people can use. Trees and rocks are both natural resources because we can use them to build houses, among other things. Natural resources are often called **raw materials**.

FOSSIL FUELS

There are a group of raw materials that are known as fossil fuels. Coal and petroleum oil are both fossil fuels that were created from the remains of plants and small sea creatures that lived millions of years ago. Over time, the plants and small sea creatures became buried in the ground and were crushed under layers of rock. This turned their remains into coal and oil.

If it is not possible to quickly make or find more of a raw material, then that raw material is said to be non-renewable. Fossil fuels are non-renewable because it takes millions of years for plant and animal remains to turn into fossil fuels, meaning that it is not possible to make more of them.

We burn fossil fuels to **generate** electricity. This process releases large amounts of harmful gases into the **atmosphere**.

COAL

Another major fossil fuel, besides coal and oil, is natural gas.

OIL

WHAT ARE
ENVIRONMENTAL ISSUES?

Environmental issues are problems that cause damage to the natural world. Environmental issues are a wide range of concerns that cover everything from air quality and pollution to saving individual **species** of animals and their **habitats**. Lots of environmental issues are caused by humans.

There is one environmental issue that many people believe is more important than the rest: air pollution. The reason people are more concerned about air pollution is because it causes so many other environmental problems. For example, climate change, acid rain and the loss of natural resources are all caused by air pollution.

Humans are using too many of the Earth's natural resources. This is causing many other environmental issues such as deforestation and water shortages. Other environmental issues, such as oil spills, are caused by accidents that could be prevented by being more careful.

Environmental issues also include any problems that negatively affect animals' habitats. Pollution, deforestation and climate change can all have terrible **consequences** for animals. In order to protect our wildlife, we must first look after the environment.

POLLUTION

WHAT IS POLLUTION?

Whenever a harmful substance is added into an environment and it causes damage, it is called pollution. Harmful substances that damage the environment are called pollutants. There are different types of pollutant as well as different types of pollution. Air pollution, water pollution and soil pollution are some of the main types.

WHAT CAUSES POLLUTION?

One of the main pollutants in today's world is carbon dioxide. Carbon dioxide can enter the atmosphere through car, factory and aeroplane **emissions**.

ACID RAIN

Acid rain is rainwater that has become **acidic**. Rainwater becomes acidic when fuel emissions react with water in the air. When acid rain falls onto fields, it can destroy **minerals** in the soil that plants need to survive.

Acid rain can also fall into rivers. This makes the water more acidic. When water becomes too acidic it can cause some species of fish to die out, which can badly affect other plants and animals living in the river. When one species of fish dies out, the **predators** that fed on it might also die out because they do not have enough to eat.

Acid rain has made many lakes in Scandinavia too acidic for fish to live in.

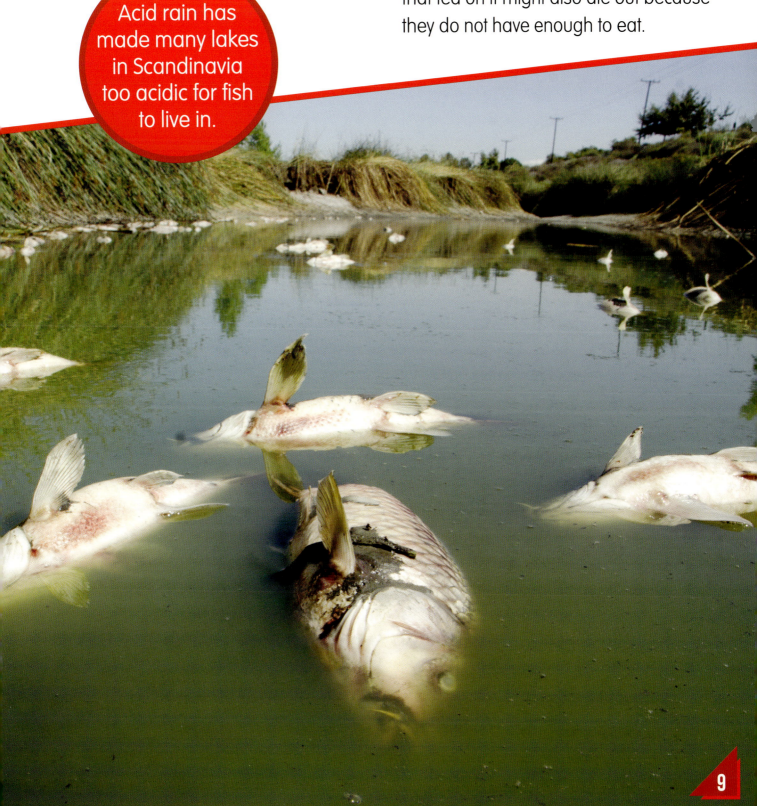

OIL SPILLS

WHAT ARE OIL SPILLS?

Oil is a fossil fuel that is found deep underground. Oil companies drill down into layers of rock to remove it, often using boats and drilling down through the bottom of the ocean. We burn oil to make electricity. We also use oil to run our cars and heat our homes.

Oil is carried from one place to another in big ships called oil tankers. Sometimes these ships accidentally spill their oil into the ocean. Oil spills can cause huge amounts of damage to the environment in a very short time. Oil cannot mix with water, meaning that when oil spills occur, the oil ends up spreading over the surface of the ocean in a thin layer.

HOW OIL SPILLS EFFECT WILDLIFE

Oil spills are especially dangerous for animals that live in the ocean, such as fish, whales and dolphins. If they swallow the oil it can poison them and cause them to die. For some animals, like sea otters and many sea birds, the oil stops them from being able to keep themselves warm, which may also cause them to die.

HOW OIL SPILLS ARE CLEANED UP

Barriers called booms are placed around oil spills to stop them from spreading. After that, skimmers are used to remove the oil. Skimmers can either be boats, vacuums or **absorbent** ropes.

POPULATION GROWTH

Earth's **population** is now over 7 billion! All these people need places to live and food to eat. Even these basic needs can put a strain on the Earth's natural resources.

The rapid expansion of cities and towns is called urbanisation. As the human population gets larger, it puts a lot of strain on resources all around the world. For example, as cities around the world get bigger and bigger, lots of forests and other natural habitats are being destroyed to make room for new buildings.

Towns and cities often replace natural landscapes. Natural landscapes are areas of land that are not man-made, such as forests and mountains. These places are important because they are home to lots of plants, trees and animals.

Towns and cities are also responsible for light pollution. Light pollution is when the night sky becomes brighter due to all of the electric lights in a town or city. Today, in some cities, the night sky can become so bright that it is impossible to see any stars at all!

The brightness of city lights means that cities are some of the only man-made things that can be seen from space.

CLIMATE CHANGE

GLOBAL WARMING

Global warming is one of today's biggest environmental issues and it is often talked about on the news. Global warming is the slow increase of the Earth's temperature caused by pollution. Global warming poses a big threat to the environment as we know it.

WHAT CAUSES IT?

Global warming is caused by **greenhouse gases** such as carbon dioxide. Normally, some of the Sun's heat bounces off the Earth and is reflected back into space, but greenhouse gases trap this heat inside the Earth's atmosphere. This causes the temperature of the planet to rise, which could lead to huge floods, long periods of drought and major crop destruction.

CLIMATE CHANGE AND POLLUTION

Most pollutants that add to air pollution, such as emissions from planes, cars and factories, lead to climate change. Carbon dioxide also comes from power stations where fossil fuels are burned to generate electricity.

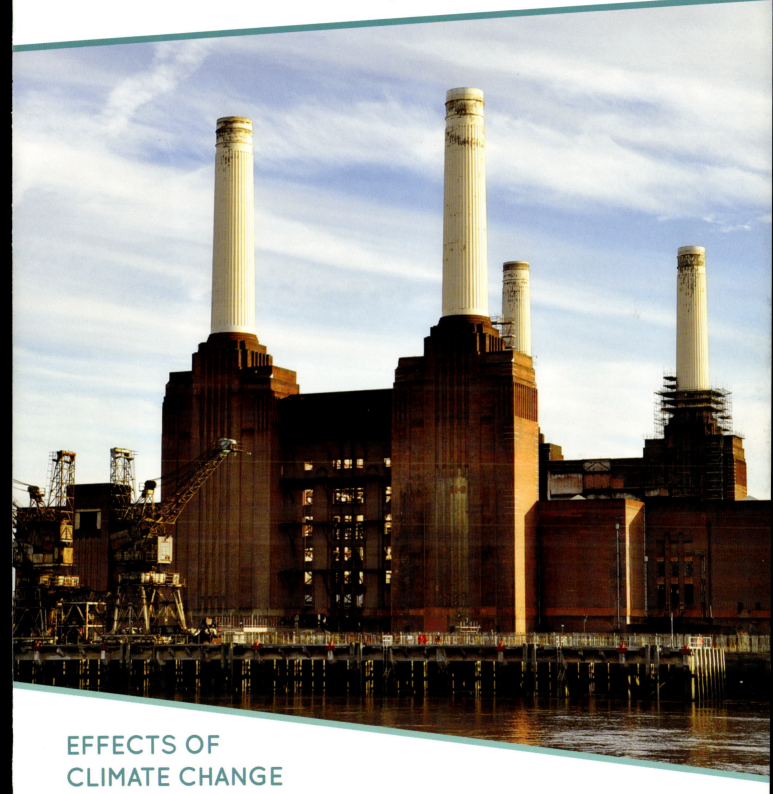

EFFECTS OF CLIMATE CHANGE

Around the North and South Poles, which are the coldest parts of our planet, there are lots of icebergs and **glaciers**. These are habitats for animals such as penguins and polar bears. Climate change causes these to melt, which leads to rising sea levels and the destruction of habitats.

DEFORESTATION

One environmental issue that is having a direct impact on wildlife is deforestation. This is where large areas of woodland are cut down, destroying many animal habitats. Trees are often cut down because they are a valuable raw material. Wood can be used to make many different things, from buildings and bridges to paper and pencils. Forests are also cut down to make room for new buildings and **infrastructure**.

Other events are also able to destroy large areas of woodland, such as forest fires. Forest fires are often caused by lightning hitting an area of very hot and dry woodland. The smoke given off by forest fires can further pollute the atmosphere, adding to air pollution.

THE AMAZON

The Amazon is a very important rainforest. It is the most heavily populated animal habitat in the world. One single tree in the Amazon can hold up to 50 different species of ant! Therefore, protecting the trees is vital to protecting the rainforest and the animals that live in it.

Many plants in the Amazon are used in medicines to cure diseases. The **medicinal properties** of many other plants in the Amazon have not yet been explored by scientists. Who knows what other diseases could be cured? If these plants are destroyed, we will never know.

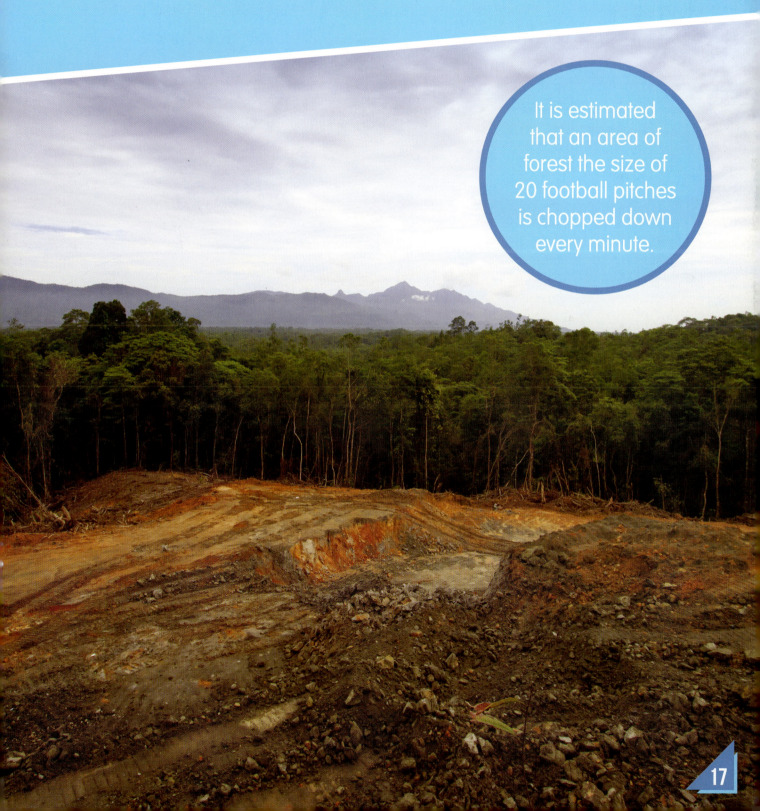

It is estimated that an area of forest the size of 20 football pitches is chopped down every minute.

WASTING WATER

Water is one of the most important resources on the planet because every living thing needs it to survive. People do not only drink water, they also use it for cooking, showering and washing clothes. 90% of the water on Earth is in the oceans, but this water is salty and not suitable for drinking. 2.5% of the water on Earth is fresh water. Fresh water is found in rivers and streams, but still only 1% of this can be used by people.

Drinking water has to be filtered and cleaned before it is drinkable. Pipes and pumps also need to be built so that the water can reach our homes. All this costs a lot of money and uses a lot of electricity.

Not all countries have the money or infrastructure to provide clean, safe water to everyone. Some people around the world have to walk great distances to their nearest water source. Women and children in some parts of rural Africa have to walk up to six kilometres to collect water.

Wasting water can affect animals too. We direct water away from rivers and streams and into farmland in order to water our crops. However, this means that there is less water in the streams, which makes it difficult for fish and plant life to survive.

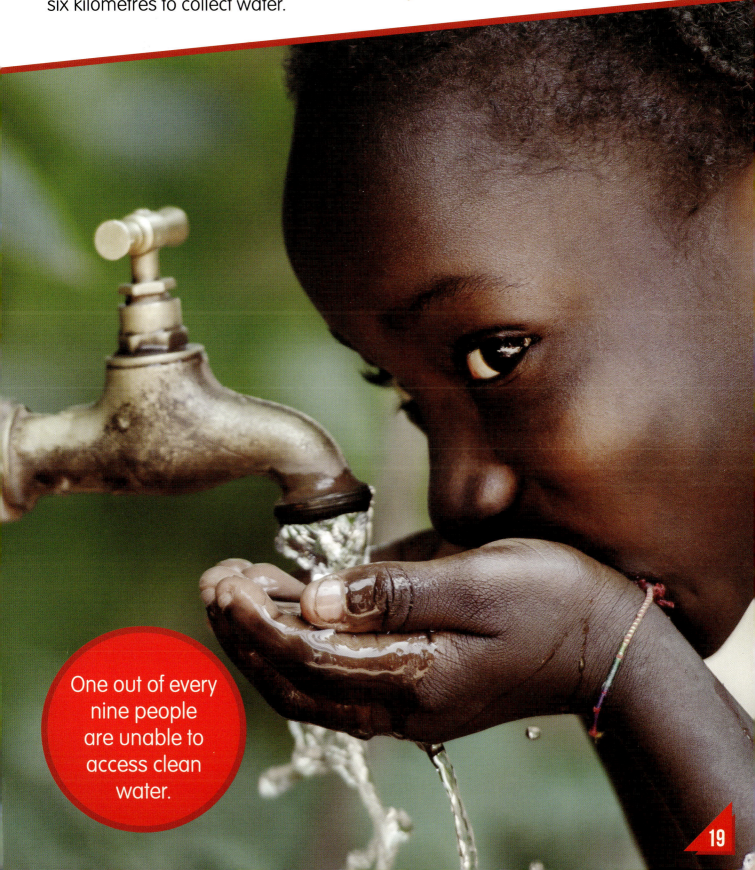

One out of every nine people are unable to access clean water.

WASTE

WHERE DOES WASTE GO?

Every hour, people in the UK throw away enough waste to fill the Royal Albert Hall. All this waste must somehow be dealt with. One of the ways that we dispose of waste is by **incineration**. This is where rubbish is burnt. However, incinerating waste often leads to lots of pollutants being released into the air, which then leads to global warming.

Waste also gets sent to landfill sites. These are big areas of land where rubbish is buried in the ground and forgotten about. Landfill sites help to get rubbish out of the way. However, as the waste **decomposes** it can release **chemicals** that pollute the air and soil.

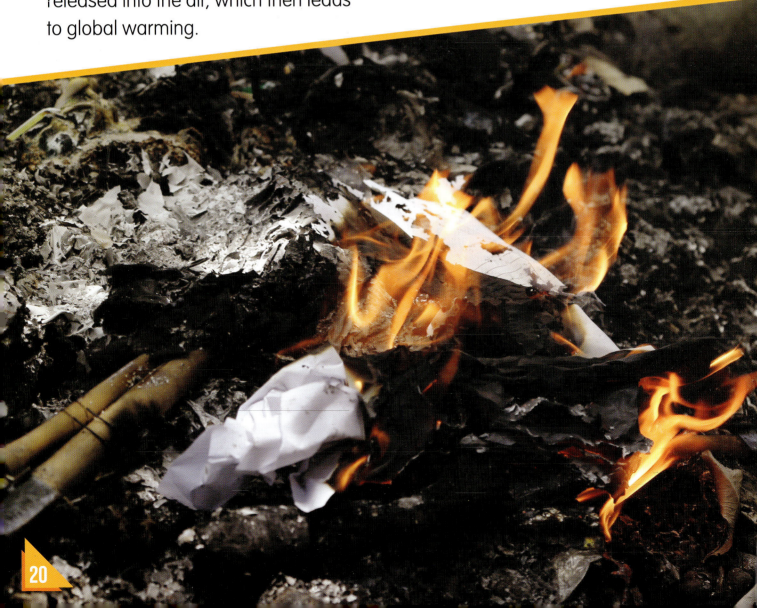

EFFECTS OF WASTE ON THE ENVIRONMENT

Some materials take much longer to decompose than others. For example, it can take plastic bags up to 1,000 years to rot away. When plastic is burned, it releases poisonous chemicals into the air. To prevent this, plastic bags are put into landfill sites. However, chemicals from the plastic bags still end up polluting the water and soil.

Humans are producing more waste now than ever before in history.

Carelessly throwing away waste can lead to serious environmental issues. For example, waste that has been dumped into the ocean has formed an island in the Pacific called 'The Great Pacific Garbage Patch'. It is estimated to be larger than Texas! This is not the only waste patch of its kind in the ocean, but it is the biggest one we know of.

WILDLIFE
IN DANGER

PENGUINS

Due to global warming, the polar ice caps are gradually melting and pieces of ice are breaking off into the sea. This poses a big threat to animals, such as penguins, that lay their eggs and look after their young on the ice caps. If global warming continues, these penguins could soon have nowhere to raise their young.

POLAR BEARS

Polar bears hunt on the ice. This means that as the ice melts away, the polar bears have less and less land on which to hunt for food.

ORANGUTANS

Orangutans are under threat from deforestation. This is because they live in forests where palms trees are being cut down for their palm oil. This oil is used in lots of different things, such as soap and toothpaste. By cutting down their natural habitat, humans are forcing the orangutans to move further into the rainforest. By forcing the orangutans deeper into the forest, we are putting them in danger. There might not be enough food for the orangutans in their new habitats and there could be different animals that make it difficult for them to survive.

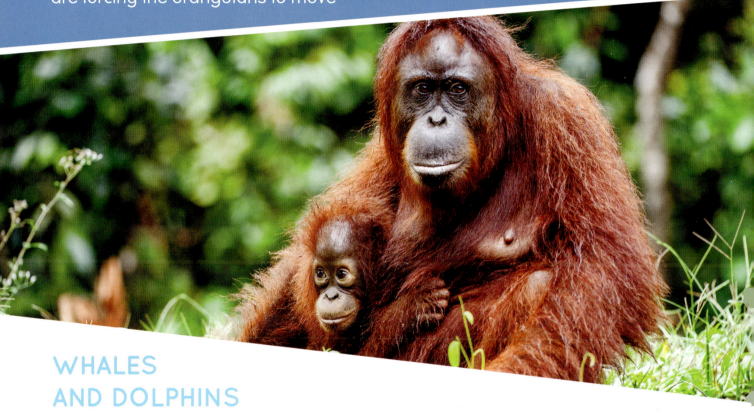

WHALES AND DOLPHINS

Ocean pollution can badly affect the lives of whales and dolphins. Whales have died after accidently eating large chunks of plastic. Dolphins sometimes get their snouts caught in rubbish that humans have dumped in the ocean. This stops them from being able to open their mouths to eat and causes them to starve to death.

269,000 tonnes of rubbish floats on the ocean's surface.

HOW CAN
WE HELP?

SAVING ENERGY

Switching off electrical items when they are not being used saves energy.
Remember that lots of fossil fuels need to be burnt to generate electricity.
The less electricity we use, the less fossil fuels need to be burnt.

HELPING WILDLIFE

If you have a garden, why not provide a green space for wildlife to live?
By planting lots of plants, you can provide a home for animals.
Remember, plants also help to reduce the amount of carbon dioxide in the air.

REDUCING FUEL EMISSIONS

A lot of air pollution comes from fuel emissions. Try to walk or cycle rather than travelling in a car. Using public transport where possible also helps reduce fuel emissions because it reduces the number of cars on the road.

SAVING WATER

We can save water by turning off the tap while we are brushing our teeth or by having a shower instead of a bath. When gardening, we can use a watering can to water plants instead of a hosepipe. This uses much less water.

REDUCE, REUSE
AND RECYCLE

One of the easiest things we can do to help the environment in our day-to-day life is to follow the three 'R's'. These are reduce, reuse and recycle.

REDUCE

We can reduce the amount of waste we throw away by:

- Buying food with less packaging.
- Not using plastic bags when we don't need to.
- Trying to buy things with recyclable packaging.

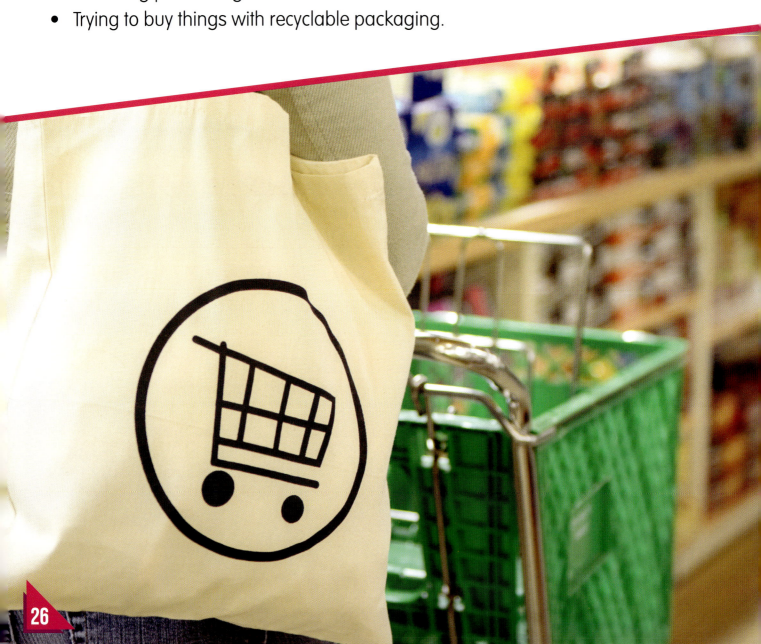

REUSE

Reuse waste by:

- Carrying shopping in reusable bags rather than plastic ones.
- Reusing old packaging by getting creative. For example, you could decorate an old yogurt pot and use it as a pen pot!
- Giving old clothes and toys to charity instead of throwing them away.

RECYCLE

When recycling always remember to:

- Only put hard plastics, glass, paper, tin, cardboard and aluminum drink cans in recycling bins.
- Rinse food waste off these materials before recycling them.
- Always check if packaging is recyclable. If it is, it will have this symbol on it:

RENEWABLE ENERGY

Reducing, reusing and recycling can help, but it will not be enough to stop climate change and protect our planet from global warming. In order to really make a difference, we need to need to use fuels that don't run out and which don't release pollutants into the environment. Thankfully, we are beginning to generate electricity using wind, sunlight and water, all of which are **renewable** sources of energy.

WIND ENERGY

Wind turbines allow us to generate electricity using the wind. Wind turbines usually have three blades that are turned by the wind. These blades are connected to a **generator**. The generator turns the energy from the spinning movement into electricity.

SOLAR ENERGY

Solar energy is energy that comes from sunlight. We can use solar cells to convert sunlight into electricity. Calculators are often powered using solar cells. Larger versions of these are called solar panels.

WATER ENERGY

Electricity can also be generated using water. This is called hydroelectric energy. A hydroelectric dam forces the water in a river to flow through a small space. This increases the speed of the flowing water. This fast-flowing water spins turbines as it passes by. A generator then turns this energy from the turbines into electricity.

QUICK QUIZ

1. What is a pollutant?

2. Which fossil fuel is often found deep in the ground under the sea?

3. What is used to clean up oil spills?

4. What can be seen from space due to light pollution?

5. Can you name three effects of global warming?

6. According to estimates, how big is the area of woodland that is cut down in the world every minute?

7. What percentage of the water on the planet is fresh water?

8. Can you name two ways to help save water?

9. Can you name an animal that is in danger of losing its habitat because of climate change?

10. Which everyday object is powered by solar cells?

GLOSSARY

absorbent	able to take in or soak up liquid
acidic	able to destroy certain materials because it contains acid
atmosphere	the mixture of gases that make up the air and surround the Earth
chemicals	substances that materials are made from
climate	the common weather conditions in a certain place
consequences	the results or effects of an action
decomposes	breaks down and rots
emissions	the harmful gases produced by cars and other vehicles
generate	create or produce electricity
generator	a machine used to convert energy into electricity
glaciers	large masses of ice that move very slowly
greenhouse gases	gases in the atmosphere that trap the Sun's heat
habitats	natural environments in which plants or animals live
incineration	the act of destroying something by burning it
infrastructure	the basic services, such as a power supply and roads, that a society needs in order to function
medicinal properties	the healing abilities of plants or other materials
minerals	important things that a plant, animal or human needs to grow
natural	relating to, existing in or made by nature
population	the amount of people living in a place
predators	animals that hunt other animals for food
raw materials	natural materials found in the environment
renewable	a resource that can be easily made or found, meaning that it will not run out

INDEX